Noble County Public Library

1. Book is due on date indicated on slip.
2. Books may be renewed by card or tele-phone.
3. A fine of 3 cents a day will be charged on books kept past due.
4. Each borrower is responsible for loss of or damage done to books drawn on his card.

EcoZones

RAIN FORESTS

Lynn M. Stone

ROURKE ENTERPRISES, INC.
Vero Beach, FL 32964

Photo Credits:

© James H. Carmichael, Jr. cover, cover inset, 27, 31, 33, 34 (bottom), 36, 37; © Robert E. Pelham 8, 15, 32, 34 (top), 42; © James P. Rowan 11, 21; © Lynn M. Stone 1, 5, 13, 17, 25, 39.

© 1989 Rourke Enterprises, Inc.

Library of Congress Cataloging in Publication Data

Stone, Lynn M.
   Rain forests / by Lynn M. Stone.
      p. cm. — (Ecozones)
   Includes index.
   Summary: Examines the rain forest as an ecological niche and describes the plant and animal life supported there.
   ISBN 0-86592-437-6
   1. Rain forest ecology — North America — Juvenile literature.
2. Rain forests — North America — Juvenile literature.   [1. Rain forest ecology.   2. Ecology.]   I. Title.   II. Series: Stone, Lynn M. Ecozones.
QH541.5.R27S76   1989
574.5'2642 — dc20   89-32746
                                                         CIP
                                                          AC

CONTENTS

RAIN FORESTS

Nowhere in North America is life more abundant than in its lush tropical rain forests. These low, wet forests are remarkably green, diverse habitats where the likes of scarlet macaws, jaguars, howler monkeys, army ants, and tapirs live among plants that stagger the imagination in number and variety. Thomas Lovejoy, an official of the Smithsonian Institution, called these tropical wonderlands the world's greatest "expression of life."

The tropical rain forests of North America are not the only type of rain forest, but they have been the topic of growing attention and concern in recent years. The tropical rain forest's remarkable plant and animal life has always amazed scientists. Now, threats to much of this forest's very existence have intensified interest in it among people outside the scientific community. According to some estimates, tropical rain forest throughout the world is being destroyed at such an alarming rate that the destroyed acreage yearly is equivalent to the size of the entire state of Pennsylvania. If that pace of destruction

Opposite *The scarlet macaw is one of several members of the parrot family that lives in Central American rain forests.*

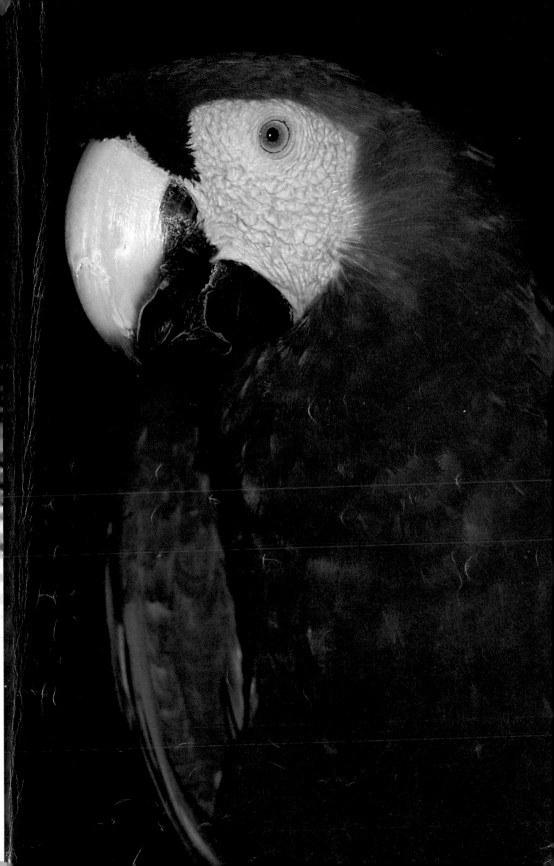

is maintained, tropical rain forest will soon be a topic more fit for history books than science books.

The idea of a steamy, leafy tropical rain forest is often associated—accurately enough—with South America, Southeast Asia, and Africa rather than North America. Actually, a fairly large portion of the **isthmus** between North America and South America is also tropical rain forest. This region is commonly known as Central America. This area, North America's "tail," and other tropical rain forest sites within North America are the focus of this book.

Scientists rarely agree on a precise definition for tropical rain forest, but the name itself is quite descriptive. First, tropical rain forest lies in the Tropic Zone, near the earth's equator. More specifically, the Tropic Zone is the region bounded by two particular parallels of latitude: the tropic of Cancer, 23½° north of the equator, and the tropic of Capricorn, 23½° south of the equator.

Rainfall is another essential characteristic of this forest type. A tropical rain forest receives at least 80 inches of rainfall each year in fairly even distribution. The most luxuriant tropical rain forests—some scientists would say the only "true" tropical rain forests— receive considerably more rainfall, sometimes as many as 400 inches.

Still another characteristic of the tropical rain forest is its vegetation. In tropical rain forests, the plant life is composed largely of tall, straight evergreen trees which form a dense canopy somewhere between 90 and 150 feet above the forest floor.

The forests of the United States, Canada, and most of Mexico are called **temperate** forests. They occur within the Temperate Zone, the region north of the Tropics and south of the Arctic Circle, which is at 66° north of the equator. Most temperate forests have an "even" appearance. You may have looked across a lakeshore and seen a fairly straight line of trees on the shore. The trees looked straight because they were all about the same height. In the tropical rain forest, the canopy forms a staggered roof for the forest; instead of being flat, it is punctuated by scattered trees called **emergents**. Their mushroom-shaped crowns tower above the main canopy and give the forest an uneven and unusual appearance.

The composition of trees in tropical and temperate forests is different, too, as

Above *Tropical rain forests are home for a remarkable variety of plants and animals.*

we would expect. The temperate forests are made up essentially of needle-leaved evergreen trees (pines, for example) and broad-leaved **deciduous** trees. The deciduous trees shed their leaves each fall and enter a **dormant** state. Their food-manufacturing processes close down for winter. The broad-leaved evergreens of the tropical rain forest don't shed all their leaves at one time because winter, as we know it, doesn't exist.

Temperate forests are usually dominated by a limited number of tree species. Tropical rain forests are thoroughly mixed, as if nature had shaken the rain forest from a blender. The patch of temperate ground that might raise 50 **species** of trees with two or three dominating species could have 300 or more tree species without any dominants in the Tropics.

The temperature of tropical rain forest is quite constant, normally between 68° F and 85° F, day and night, year-round. The heat, rain, and water vapor released from plants produce humidity, or dampness, in the air. Humidity is another constant of the tropical rain forest. During the day, the air in a tropical rain forest averages 70 percent humidity, or moisture saturation. At night, the humidity climbs to 95 percent.

Most of North America's tropical rain forest is in southern Mexico and along the eastern and northern coasts of Central America. Its most luxuriant growth is slightly inland at altitudes of 300 to 600 feet above sea level. A few smaller tracts are on the Pacific coast of Costa Rica, Guatemala, and Chiapas, Mexico. There are also rain forests, somewhat influenced by temperate climate, in Cuba, Haiti, the Dominican Republic, Puerto Rico, and other Caribbean islands.

The central portion of the tropical rain forest in the Americas covers the Orinoco and Amazon River basins in northern and central South America. The rain forests beyond that region, including those in Central America, don't achieve the same extremes of variety and lushness that characterizes the South American forests.

Tropical rain forest is not strictly a feature of North and South America. Tropical rain forests occur, generally on large land masses within the Tropic Zone, in parts of Asia, Australia, and Africa. These rain forests are not identical to those of the Americas, but they share the same kind of climate and ecological **niches**, or roles. For instance, the role of **predator** that the jaguar has in the forests of the Americas is similar to the leopard's role in the tropical rain forest of the Malay Peninsula.

Looking at the tropical rain forest from above reveals a lumpy, dark green canopy broken by the protruding emergents. Seeing the tropical rain forest from within is an altogether different experience. The visitor is immediately impressed, even at midday, by how little light penetrates the canopy to the forest floor or litter level. The sky, it seems, has disappeared. A visitor is also impressed by the ever present heat and humidity, and by the surprising openness of the forest. The openness is the

consequence of the canopy, a giant solar panel that does wonders for the tall trees but little for the forest ground floor. With only flecks and occasional needle beams of sunlight reaching the forest bottom, green plants, dependent upon the radiant energy of the sun for their food production, do not grow densely.

In the dim, green light of day, the tropical rain forest is still and quiet. The canopy absorbs most of the wind, and there is little disturbance from large animals. Many animals tend to be active at night; anyway, there is little on the forest floor for large animals to eat. Much of the wildlife activity, and the squawks and shrieks of parrots and monkeys, occurs out of sight high in the canopy overhead.

Above *Tree ferns (center left) and epiphytes on trees (left and center) are characteristic of tropical rain forest.*

2 TYPES OF RAIN FOREST

The tropical rain forest has numerous variations, far more than scientists have been able to study. Different soils account for some variations, and changing altitudes and latitudes account for others. The Caribbean island rain forests, for example, are far enough north to be shaped by the temperate climate and different rain patterns than those that hammer the true **equatorial** forests.

In mountainous areas of Central America, the lowland rain forests often gradually become cloud forests. The average temperature drops three to four degrees Fahrenheit for each 1,000 feet of altitude, and temperature affects which plant species can survive. At 3,000 feet above sea level, the forest that began in the hot lowlands has experienced a drop of somewhere between ten and twelve degrees. The variety of species has been reduced, new species have moved in, and the overall tree height has declined. Leaves are smaller and the characteristic layering, or **stratification**, of rain forest plants is not nearly as evident.

Opposite The cougar is the only mammal species to be found in both tropical and temperate rain forests.

What had been a tropical rain forest has become a cloud forest. Cloud forests are wet, certainly. Between 3,000 and 5,000 feet above sea level, they bathe in almost daily cloud cover as well as in frequent rains. But they are colder than tropical rain forests, have less light because of the sun-smothering clouds, and almost year-round humidity saturation. Trees are denser here than at lower altitudes, but they are also shorter.

TROPICAL RAIN FORESTS

CLOUD FOREST

TROPICAL RAIN FOREST

Ferns, mosses, and liverworts are so thick on the branches of cloud forest trees that these forests are sometimes known as "moss forests."

Eventually the mountain slopes and peaks extend beyond the belts of clouds. With increasing cold and decreasing moisture, trees yield to stunted shrubs, grasses, and numerous other soft-bodied plants, most of which bear no resemblance to the green plants of the humid lowlands.

The temperate rain forest of the Pacific Northwest should not be confused with the tropical rain forest, the central theme of this book. Nevertheless,

Above *The golden toad is restricted to certain Costa Rican cloud forests.*

the temperate rain forest is a region of tremendous beauty and interest, and it shares some traits with the tropical forests of North America. From the southern edge of the temperate rain forest zone to the northern reach of tropical rain forest is about 1,500 miles. Still, distance aside, the rain forests of North and South share a major similarity: an abundance of rain. The temperate rain forests receive more than 80 inches of rainfall each year and the tropical rain forests as many as 200 inches.

The temperate rain forests of North America occur from northern California north some 2,500 miles to Kodiak Island, Alaska. They are part of a coastal corridor of largely needle-leaved trees dominated by western red cedar, Sitka spruce, and western hemlock. The region as a whole has an average rainfall of 50 to 100 inches per year. The wettest sections of this zone, usually occurring at modest altitudes fairly near the coast, are exceptionally lush. They represent the finest examples of temperate rain forest.

The temperate rain forests are much colder than the tropical forests. Indeed, the average temperature along much of the dark, brooding Alaska shore, where some of the best rain forest stands, is about 40° F. The plant and animal species of the tropical and temperate rain forests are virtually all different, and the rainfall distribution is different. The heartland of the tropical rain forest zone has fairly even distribution of rain throughout the year. The temperate rain forests have more pronounced rainy seasons and dry seasons. Another difference is the soil, which is deeper and richer in the temperate forests.

The largest North American rain forests in the Temperate Zone are in Southeast Alaska. Tongass National Forest is the centerpiece of the Alaskan

Below *Olympic National Park is the site of four lush, mossy temperate rain forests. Hoh River rain forest is shown here.*

rain forest. Several designated wilderness areas and two national monuments, Admiralty Island and Misty Fjords, within the 16-million acres of the Tongass have substantial rain forests.

The best-known temperate rain forests are the most easily accessible. These are the rain forests of Olympic National Park in Washington State. Four rain forests in the park—Hoh, Queets, Quinalt, and Bogachiel—have developed in river valleys facing west or southwest. The prevailing west winds from the Pacific Ocean tote moisture straight up the river valleys. Soaked and sheltered, the valleys produce mighty Sitka spruce, western red cedar, western hemlock, and scattered Douglas fir trees. These pillars of the forest stand up to 200 feet. Below them is a layer of mostly deciduous trees dominated by big leaf maples about 60 feet tall. The ground story, the third level in the layers of this temperate rain forest, is a tangle of mossy logs, ferns, vine maple, and berry bushes. Moss grows in profusion on the ground, on tree trunks, and on branches. Twigs trail ribbons of moss and main limbs disappear under moss gardens.

Nature spent lavishly here, as she did in the tropical rain forest. But the effect is subdued in the quiet, damp grandeur of massive trees and arching, moss-draped branches. The vegetation lends a hush and acts as natural, misty green insulation from the outside world. Rain doesn't so much pelt the forest understory as drip on it.

The Olympic rain forests are visited by Roosevelt elk, whose grazing and browsing habits help keep some of the forest understory trimmed. Farther north, the temperate rain forests are the home of Sitka deer, relatives of the elk. Black bears are found throughout the temperate rain forests, but they rarely prey on elk or deer. During summers at least, salmon and berries are much easier for the bears to corner. The major predator of deer and elk is the cougar, or mountain lion. The cougar is the only mammal of the temperate rain forests that also can be found occasionally in the tropical rain forests, where it preys on white-tailed deer and brocket deer.

THE MAKING
OF THE RAIN FOREST

Tropical rain forests, in one form or another, have existed for millions of years. Their size has ebbed and flowed with the climate changes of past ages. During wet, warm interludes in **geologic time**, the tropical rain forests spread. During cold times, they shrank to a few, isolated pockets. These islands of tropical rain forest, according to one scientific theory, are the reason that the life of the rain forests is so diversified. The isolation of rain forest pockets prompted **evolution** of new plant and animal species, or at least changes in existing species. When a population of frogs, for example, was separated by climatic upheavals, each population, over thousands of years, changed in different ways from the other. Eventually, when the rain forests blended into a large body of land, each of the formerly isolated pockets contributed its own unique cast of plants and animals. The "new" species found interbreeding blocked by physical or behavioral differences.

The climate of the equatorial region maintains the tropical rain forests. Along the equatorial lowlands,

Opposite *Heavy rains pelt tropical rain forests throughout much of the year. (El Yunque Rain Forest, Puerto Rico)*

consistently high temperatures are the rule, partly because the sun is potentially available to shine 12 hours each day, year-round. The sun's rays strike the equator at right angles, and that creates heightened intensity of sunlight, another factor in producing high temperatures and healthy plants. Heat and rainfall contribute to the characteristic high humidity of tropical rain forests, and unceasing rains influence the poor soil. All of these factors produce the environment in which typical rain forest plants thrive. Where the appropriate land elevation, soil, humidity, and rainfall are not present, tropical rain forest does not develop. Because a location falls within the Tropic Zone doesn't necessarily mean that it is rain forest. Several environmental circumstances, such as volcanic soil and high altitude, can stifle the growth of tropical rain forest.

PLANTS OF THE RAIN FOREST

Because tropical rain forest soil is generally poor, it seems unlikely that plants would thrive in it. Nevertheless, the rain forest is a showplace of green plants.

The soil of the tropical rain forest is poor because it is short on **nutrients**. Nutrients are the elements that nourish living organisms. Rain brings some nutrients with it, but it also washes nutrients in the soil away when it falls in the volume that it does in the Tropics. In addition, tropical rain forest soils are relatively old, so their mineral content is somewhat exhausted from countless generations of forest. The trees in the rain forest compensate for the poor soil quality by growing shallow roots. When dead plants and animals decay, they are a major source of nutrients, and shallow roots absorb considerable nutrition before the rains can wash it away.

The trees of the tropical rain forest grow in fairly consistent layers, or **strata**. Looking at the forest from within doesn't reveal the stratified character of the woods, because one layer tends to obscure the next.

The highest level of the tropical rain forest is the height reached by the tallest trees, the emergents, which usually top 150 feet and occasionally reach 200. The emergents do not form a canopy layer because there are only one or two of them per acre.

Below the emergents is the forest canopy, a mesh of leaves, branches, and tangling vines. The canopy tends to be composed of trees that are 60 to 90 feet tall and have rounded crowns. The canopy catches most of the sunlight. Sunlight that filters down below the canopy falls mostly on the forest understory, a layer of flame-shaped tree crowns between 15 and 45 feet tall.

Seedlings, **herbs**, and ferns grow on the forest floor, but the lack of available sunlight keeps this area quite open. The fact that heat and humidity accelerate decay has reduced the expected litter of logs, twigs, and leaves.

The hundreds of tree species that help make the tropical rain forest such a diverse environment are themselves a somewhat uniform group, despite having such delightful names as banak, ironwood, cohune, waika plum, negrito, cacho vennado, monkey tail, and kerosene wood. Almost all of the forest tree leaves are less than six inches long.

Opposite *Orchids are common in tropical rain forests. Biologists claim to know more than 1,000 species in Costa Rica alone.*

They are leathery, glossy dark green, somewhat narrow, and pointed. The points are called "drip tips." Scientists suspect that the tips help the leaves rid themselves quickly of rain drops. Lingering water would stimulate the growth of tiny plants that could injure the leaves. A notable exception to the small leaves of tropical rain forest trees is the corozo palm with its 30-foot leaves.

Tree trunks of the tropical rain forest typically have thin bark that looks quite similar from one species to the next. A few trees among the emergents and upper canopy have stilted or buttressed trunks. Buttressed trunks are thicker closer to the base. Sometimes they are massive. Scientists aren't sure what the advantage of these structural deviations is, although some scientists think they offer the tree additional support.

If the trees tend to be somewhat monotonous, the other plant species more than compensate. Dangling liana vines and other climbers, standard features in tropical rain forest, can grow as thick as a man's leg. Ferns are plentiful, and some are woody-stemmed, allowing them to grow to tree size. In fact, half the plant species of tropical rain forests

are woody. The lateral branches of trees, tree crotches, and rough bark are colonized by remarkable populations of ferns, mosses, orchids, and bromeliads. Tree limbs frequently break from the overload of their lush hanging gardens of **epiphytes**.

Epiphytes are the ferns, mosses, orchids, bromeliads, and other plants that grow on plants, usually trees. Epiphytes use another plant for their structural support. They attach themselves to the host plant by a root system of various proportions, but epiphytes do not feed on the host as a **parasite** would.

Above *Buttressed roots may give tall rain forest trees additional support.*

Normally, the host plant is unharmed by the epiphytes.

Epiphytes must take their nutrients from air, water, and whatever **detritus** they may collect. Some epiphytes have cup-like bases from which a series of long, pointed leaves spread. The "cups" become miniature reservoirs and a habitat for tree frogs, lizards, snakes, and other creatures that are looking for an aquatic home above ground or just a drink of fresh water. Certain tree frogs lay eggs in the reservoirs of epiphytes.

The most dazzling of the epiphytes are the many orchid species. Costa Rican **biologists** claim that Costa Rica alone has over 1,000 species of orchid, many of them perched on trees and producing the broad, bright blossoms reminiscent of corsages.

Plants of the tropical rain forest require **pollination** as part of their reproductive process. Pollination occurs with the transfer of pollen grains from a flower's stamen to its stigma. There are several means of pollination, including the wind. But wind is too chancy in much of the tropical rain forest. Most winds are deflected by the forest canopy, and most plant species tend to be too widely separated from each other to enable wind to be a likely pollinator.

Therefore, much of the pollinating is unknowingly undertaken by animals. Hummingbirds, bats, and insects visit various flowers for nectar, a sweet plant secretion. In exchange for having parted with its nectar, the flower is pollinated as the animal travels from one flower to another.

Animals are also important in dispersing plant seeds. Specific birds are drawn to certain brightly colored fruits, and bats and other animals are attracted to fruits with distinct odors. The animals digest the fleshy part of the plant's fruit and pass the seeds through their digestive systems. Thus dispersed, the seeds may take root in their new surroundings.

5 ANIMALS OF THE RAIN FOREST

A myth about the tropical rain forest is that it is teeming with large, exotic mammals like some tropical Noah's ark. Actually, comparatively few large animals range through the tropical rain forest floors. The foliage is too high for browsing animals and there is virtually no grass for grazers. **Terrestrial** mammals have to eat **microorganisms**, ground plants, litter, or fallen fruits. Most of the relatively large ground animals that do live in the tropical rain forest of North America are **herbivorous**, or plant-eaters. The largest among them is the endangered Baird's tapir, a hoofed animal with a long, sloped snout. White-tailed deer, the smaller brocket deer, peccaries, and two heavyweight rodents—the agouti and paca—are also among the forest herbivores.

Because of the scarcity of herbivores, the meat-eating **carnivores** are not plentiful either, although armadillos, which live primarily on insect and other **invertebrates**, are fairly common. Another insect-eating creature of the region is the giant anteater. The dominant predator of the American rain

Opposite *The rainbow lizard is one of several brightly colored reptiles found in the tropical rain forest.*

Above *Three-toed sloths move slowly through tropical rain forest canopy, sometimes hanging upside down.*

forests is the jaguar, a large, spotted cat that may weigh well over 200 pounds. Jaguars often follow river courses; they are very much at home in the water. The jaguar can kill virtually anything it finds. Its main prey is agouti, armadillo, deer, and peccary.

Among the **arboreal**, or tree dwelling, mammals of our tropical rain forest are porcupines, many species of bats, opossums, mice, kinkajous, coatis, monkeys, squirrels, and sloths. Two small spotted cats, the **endangered** margay and ocelot, also live there. Not all of these animals spend their entire life cycle above ground, but each is part of

the rain forest's upper layers for substantial time.

Just as many mammals have discovered the advantages of life at the top, so have many of the tropical rain forest's other animals. The foliage, fruit, and plant debris that collects on limbs and in tree crotches are rich food sources and powerful magnets for animals. Insects—bees, ants, dragonflies, moths, katydids, butterflies—live above the forest floor in abundance along with other invertebrates like cockroaches, scorpions, centipedes, and spiders. The trails of animals line the beds of moss on tree limbs.

Above *White-faced capuchin monkeys live in tree tops of Central American rain forests.*

Right *A vivid morpho butterfly in Costa Rica appears to have been cut from blue plastic wrap.*

Right *The keel-billed toucan, nicknamed "banana bill," uses its bill to crush fruit.*

Few birds live on the ground, but scores of them live in the heights. Depending on a particular species, rain forest birds feed on fruit, nectar, seeds, insects, mammals, reptiles, and amphibians. The birds of the tropical rain forest include some familiar names from temperate forests—hummingbirds, flycatchers, tanagers, owls, hawks, woodpeckers, and others. Some of the exclusively tropical residents are macaws, parrots, toucans, and parakeets.

Each bird fits a particular niche and pursues a food source that doesn't conflict with another bird's food source. Among the hummingbirds, for example, the long-billed starthroat hummingbird sips nectar while pollinating flowers. The short-billed Jacobin snatches flying insects. The purple-crowned humming-bird picks spiders from the undersides of leaves.

The trees are also home for a variety of reptiles and amphibians. A few of them are the giant iguana, the common boa constrictor, the horned palm viper, which dangles from vines and snares passing birds, and numerous, vividly colored tree frogs.

Tree frogs of temperate North America are well known for their protective coloration. They match their surroundings almost faultlessly. Some of their tropical relatives in the rain forest are equally skilled at camouflage. But other tree frogs of the Tropics are among the most brightly colored creatures on earth. Nature has painted them in bold colors as a warning that they are extremely poisonous to the touch and certainly to the stomach.

Above *This Honduran milk snake is one of numerous snakes in the tropical rain forest. The milk snake is harmless, but several rain forest snakes are not.*

Some of the Indians in South America have traditionally dipped their darts and hunting arrows into the poisons which they have extracted from tree frogs. The frogs have appropriately been named dart-poison and arrow-poison frogs. The poisons are in the frogs' skins, not in their mouths. The poison is used to deter predators, not to kill insects, the frogs' prey.

One of the most conspicuous animals of the tropical rain forest is also one of the smallest—the ant. Ants in the rain forest come in various descriptions. One of the most interesting varieties is the leaf-cutter. Leaf-cutter ants bring leaf fragments to their nests. The ants

leave the fragments alone until they have borne a fungus. It is the fungus that the ants eat.

Army ants are equally fascinating. Some species move in single file. Others advance in waves, sending scouts ahead. Army ants have a frightening reputation—like the piranha fish of tropical streams—but it's somewhat exaggerated. The bites of hundreds of army ants can immobilize large animals, and army ants have killed tethered livestock. But the legions of hundreds of thousands of marching army ants move very slowly. They are not likely to be a threat to humans.

Above *The arrow-poison tree frog warns predators away with its colorful hues.*

6

THE FLOW OF ENERGY

Energy is necessary for plants and animals to live and function in their environment. Animals spend much of their lives locating energy in the form of food, which, in one way or another, comes from plants. Plants manufacture, or produce, food. In a system of interrelated plants and animals, such as a tropical rain forest, the energy flows from one living organism to another in a series of **food chains**.

Food chains begin with the manufacture of food by plants in a process known as **photosynthesis**. The plants' ability to use sunlight in the process is critical.

In addition to sunlight, most green plants need carbon dioxide, water, and minerals from the soil to produce food and grow. As you know, these minerals are scarce in the tropical rain forest soil, but shallow roots quickly help plants absorb the minerals that are released from decaying plants and animals. Scientists think that among the billions of invisible organisms that live in the soil are some special fungi, a very simple but important family of plants. They

Opposite *The armadillo, one of comparatively few mammals on the rain forest floor, takes food energy from insects and other invertebrates.*

presumably provide tree roots with an accelerated flow of nutrients, speeding the process by which roots absorb minerals.

As in any community of plants and animals, each organism, large and small, is sooner or later food for another organism. The herbivores consume plant material, releasing for themselves some of the energy stored in the plant. The carnivores eat herbivores and other, smaller carnivores. The energy originally stored in the plant, then, moves through a series, or chain, of animal consumers. Even the largest, most powerful carnivores ultimately die and are quickly processed by the forest **decomposers**. The decomposers are mostly microorganisms, fungi and bacteria, which release the nutrients in the dead animal back into the air and soil. Whatever the precise reasons may be, the tropical rain forest quickly and continually recycles these nutrients. In doing so, it maintains an efficient ecosystem in which each species prospers as energy flows from one to the other.

CONSERVATION OF THE RAIN FOREST

The temperate rain forests of North America have been gradually disappearing along the Pacific coast. Old growth forests in the rainy zone are prized for lumber. One of the best indicators of old growth destruction in Oregon and Washington has been the corresponding disappearance of the northern spotted owl. This bird seems incapable of living anywhere except in old growth forest. It has recently been named a **threatened species** by the U.S. Fish and Wildlife Service. That designation may help protect remaining old growth forests from destruction as the government tries to protect remaining spotted owls.

In Alaska, the Tongass National Forest, containing rain forest in massive proportion, has long been a battleground for environmentalists and the timber industry with the National Forest Service in the middle. The issue is which, if any, of the spectacular old growth sections of the forest should be cut.

But the future of North America's temperate rain forests is much brighter than that of its tropical rain forests. Central America has abused her forests

Above *Destruction of the tropical rain forest for logging and agriculture in Central America and elsewhere threatens the existence of many rain forest tracts.*

for generations. As long ago as 1909, a visitor to Central America wrote, "Truly virgin forests seem not to exist in Central America. Relicts of ancient agriculture occupations seem nowhere to be lacking."

Much of the abuse has centered on slash-and-burn agriculture. That practice involves cutting rain forest, burning the trees, and planting crops. In moderation, slash-and-burn farming made little impact on the forest as a whole, but as the populations of Central American nations have expanded, slash-and-burn agriculture has made inroads on the tropical rain forests.

For poor farmers and those people

fleeing the poverty of cities, clearing the rain forest seems like a wise investment of energy. The trouble is, slash-and-burn agriculture has no long-term future. Rain forest sites make poor cropland after a few plantings. The soil is thin and nutrient-poor. Furthermore, without the forest cover, the land easily erodes in heavy downpours and washes into otherwise clean streams and rivers.

Slash-and-burn agriculture is not the only reason for increased rain forest **deforestation**. Demand for products that can be grown on former rain forest sites, however briefly, has also contributed to the disappearance of rain forests. Among those products are coffee, bananas, rubber, palm hearts, and cattle. Some of the trees themselves are in demand for their lumber value.

Developed countries like the United States and Canada have contributed to the decline of the tropical rain forest by financing projects that involve highway construction, dams, and large-scale agriculture. Many of these projects have short-term advantages for people, but questionable futures. It seems apparent that the destruction of rain forests may have far more serious consequences than the loss of trees and wildlife habitat.

For one thing, rain forest destruction may deprive everyone of potential food sources, medicines, and other products. Our knowledge of the rain forest is sketchy. We will never have a chance to unlock the rain forest's secrets at its current rate of destruction.

Rain forest destruction may even affect weather. The rain forest adds a tremendous amount of moisture to the air as excess water evaporates from leaves. The moisture eventually becomes rain. Some areas have already experienced droughts attributed to the loss of forest.

Rain forest wildlife has suffered from the loss of habitat, but also from animal collectors who have taken thousands and thousands of monkeys, parrots, macaws, iguanas, and ocelots from the Central American rain forests. The plight of the forest and its wildlife is not encouraging, but there are a few positive signs.

Perhaps the most positive sign comes from Costa Rica. While its Central American neighbors and the countries in South America have generally ignored rain forest conservation, Costa Rica has aggressively set aside large tracts of its wilderness since 1969. Its study sites and research teams have been in the forefront of rain forest scholarship.

Belize, another country in Central America, has set aside the Cockscomb Basin Jaguar Preserve, thanks to the field studies of Alan Abramowitz and the New York Zoological Society. This preserve is an effort to protect one of the continent's most powerful and beautiful predators.

Research has not kept pace with destruction, but scientists are busy trying to find alternatives to the wholesale wrecking of rain forest ecosystems. The development of tourism, if handled properly, could provide livelihoods for those who would otherwise make their living by slash-and-burn agriculture. In Brazil, scientists are working to determine the minimum size necessary to protect intact a tropical rain forest ecosystem.

The rain forest is like a bottomless crater of pulsing life, and we know so little about it. If we do not soon find creative alternatives to the destruction of tropical rain forests, the rain forest's secrets will be lost forever. Even now, they are escaping in plumes of white smoke and in muddy streams racing through eroded lands once lush and green.

GLOSSARY

arboreal   tree-dwelling

biologist   one who studies living organisms

carnivore   meat-eating animal

deciduous   a plant that periodically loses its leaves; typically, broad-leaved trees in the autumn

decomposer   an organism, most often bacteria and fungi, that consumes dead tissue and reduces it to small particles

deforestation   the removal of forest growth

detritus   tiny particles of decaying plants and animals

dormant   referring to a plant or animal in a state of inactivity due to the slowing or stopping of normal functions

emergent   a tree of the tropical rain forest that grows well above the forest canopy

endangered species   a kind of animal which is in danger of extinction

epiphyte   a plant which grows on another plant and gathers its nourishment from air and rain; an air plant

equatorial   of or relating to the earth's equator

evolution   in plant and animal life, a process of gradual change or development

food chain   the transfer of energy from green plants through a series of consuming animals

geologic time   the lengthy period of time relating to the history of the earth

herb   a flowering plant with a soft rather than woody stem

herbivorous   referring to an animal that eats plants

invertebrate   an animal without a backbone

isthmus   a narrow strip of land connecting two larger land areas

microorganism   a microscopic organism invisible to the naked eye

niche   an organism's role or job in the community

nutrient   a substance providing a living organism with nourishment

parasite   a organism that lives for its own benefit on or in another organism, which it harms

photosynthesis   the process by which green plants produce simple food sugars through the use of sunlight and chlorophyll

pollination   the transfer of pollen from a flower's stamen to its stigma

predator   an animal that kills and feeds on other animals

species   a group of plants or animals whose members reproduce naturally only with other plants or animals of the same group; a particular kind of plant or animal, such as a jaguar or golden toad

strata   layers that are part of a whole, as in the layers of forest

stratification   the condition of being in layers or strata

temperate   referring to that part of the earth in the Northern Hemisphere between the tropic of Cancer at 23½° north of the equator and the Arctic Circle at 66° north of the equator

terrestrial   ground-dwelling

threatened species   a kind of animal whose population has been reduced and which may eventually be in danger of extinction

46

RAIN FOREST SITES

The following is a list of sites where you can expect to find characteristic plants and animals of the rain forests and outstanding rain forest scenery:

COSTA RICA

Braulio Carrillo National Park, San Jose (cloud forest)
Corcovado National Park, Nicoya
Manuel Antonio National Park, Quepos
Monteverde Cloud Forest Preserve, San Jose
Tortuguero National Park, Tortuguero

GUATEMALA

Ixcán National Park, Huehuetenango

PANAMA

Frontenzo National Park, Panama City

PUERTO RICO

Caribbean National Forest, Palmer

UNITED STATES (Temperate Rain Forests)

Alaska
Tongass National Forest, Juneau, Alaska
Washington
Olympic National Park, Port Angeles, Washington

ACTIVITIES

Here are some activities and projects that will help you learn more about the North American tropical rain forests:

1. Draw a map of North America and show the extent of both tropical and temperate rain forests, or concentrate on the tropical rain forests in Mexico, Central America, and the Caribbean Sea. Illustrate your map with drawings or pictures of typical rain forest plants and animals, such as jaguars, macaws, morpho butterflies, and monkeys.

2. Design a travel brochure for a particular rain forest. Describe the area's plants, animals, and scenic value. Tell what clothes would be appropriate and why. Tell how to reach the area and how someone would get around once there. Why would people want to go there? What would they be able to do there?

3. Compare the tropical rain forests of Central and perhaps South America with the tropical rain forests of Asia, Australia, or Africa. You could also compare the tropical rain forests of North America with the temperate rain forests.

4. Create a collage of rain forest plants and animals.

5. Join a conservation organization that promotes the protection of rain forest plants, animals, and wilderness. Several national and international organizations are listed here:

The Basic Foundation
P.O. Box 47012
St. Petersburg, FL 33700

National Wildlife Federation
1400 16th St., NW
Washington, DC 20036-2266

The Nature Conservancy
1815 N. Lynn St.
Arlington, VA 22209

World Wildlife Fund
Conservation Foundation
1250 24th St., NW
Washington, DC 20037

INDEX

Numbers in boldface type refer to photo pages.